D1487495

LARRY FITZGERALD

Russell Roberts

Mitchell Lane
PUBLISHERS

P.O. Box 196
Hockessin, Delaware 19707
Visit us on the web: www.mitchelllane.com
Comments? email us: mitchelllane@mitchelllane.com

Mitchell Lane

PUBLISHERS

Copyright © 2011 by Mitchell Lane Publishers. All rights reserved. No part of this book may be reproduced without written permission from the publisher. Printed and bound in the United States of America.

Printing   1   2   3   4   5   6   7   8   9

A Robbie Reader
Contemporary Biography

Abigail Breslin	Albert Pujols	Alex Rodriguez
Aly and AJ	Amanda Bynes	AnnaSophia Robb
Ashley Tisdale	Brenda Song	Brittany Murphy
Charles Schulz	Dakota Fanning	Dale Earnhardt Jr.
David Archuleta	Demi Lovato	Donovan McNabb
Drake Bell & Josh Peck	Dr. Seuss	Dwayne "The Rock" Johnson
Dylan & Cole Sprouse	Eli Manning	Emily Osment
Emma Watson	Hilary Duff	Jaden Smith
Jamie Lynn Spears	Jennette McCurdy	Jesse McCartney
Jimmie Johnson	Johnny Gruelle	Jonas Brothers
Jordin Sparks	Justin Bieber	Keke Palmer
Larry Fitzgerald	LeBron James	Mia Hamm
Miley Cyrus	Miranda Cosgrove	Raven-Symoné
Selena Gomez	Shaquille O'Neal	Story of Harley-Davidson
Syd Hoff	Taylor Lautner	Tiki Barber
Tom Brady	Tony Hawk	Victoria Justice

Library of Congress Cataloging-in-Publication Data
Roberts, Russell, 1953–
  Larry Fitzgerald / by Russell Roberts.
    p. cm. — (A Robbie reader)
  Includes bibliographical references and index.
  ISBN 978-1-58415-899-8 (library bound)
  1. Fitzgerald, Larry, 1983– —Juvenile literature. 2. Football players—United States—
Biography—Juvenile literature. 3. Arizona Cardinals (Football team)—Juvenile literature.
I. Title.
  GV939.F55R63 2011
  796.332092—dc22
  [B]
                                                                                  2010014902

ABOUT THE AUTHOR: Russell Roberts has written and published nearly 40 books for adults and children on a variety of subjects, including baseball, memory power, business, New Jersey history, and travel. He has written numerous books for Mitchell Lane Publishers, including *Holidays and Celebrations in Colonial America*, *What's So Great About Daniel Boone*, *The Life and Times of Nostradamus*, *Poseidon*, and *The Cyclopes*. He lives in Bordentown, New Jersey, with his family and a fat, fuzzy, and crafty calico cat named Rusti.

TABLE OF CONTENTS

Words in **bold** type can be found in the glossary.

Larry "Sticky Fingers" Fitzgerald is one of the best wide receivers in professional football. He tears for the goal line in the 2009 Super Bowl versus the Pittsburgh Steelers.

The Big Game

Sixty-three yards from the goal line, **quarterback** (KWOR-ter-bak) Kurt Warner threw the football downfield. **Wide receiver** (ree-SEE-ver) Larry Fitzgerald streaked ahead of it. He caught the ball on the run and raced toward the end zone. Touchdown!

Fitzgerald did not **spike** the ball or show off. He raised the ball high, then handed it to an **official** (oh-FIH-shul). Even though he was playing in the **Super Bowl**, he was as polite as ever.

His team, the Arizona Cardinals, was under a lot of pressure. Their **opponents** (uh-POH-nunts) were the Pittsburgh Steelers. The Steelers had won five Super Bowls before. The

Cardinals never had. During the regular season, the Steelers had won 12 games. The Cardinals had won only 9. Many people thought the Cardinals didn't stand a chance.

They thought wrong. Fitzgerald's touchdown put the Cardinals ahead 23-20.

With the football cradled in his arm, Larry races for the end zone as the Steelers defense gives chase. A good wide receiver needs speed to be able to outrun the defensive backs.

There were only 2 minutes and 37 seconds left to play. The Cardinals were close to doing what no one thought they could do. They were about to defeat the mighty Steelers.

Fitzgerald had done a lot to help the Cardinals get to the Super Bowl. In the playoffs, he had caught 23 passes for 419 yards and five touchdowns. He broke **National Football League** (NFL) records set by Jerry Rice, one of the best wide receivers in NFL history. "[Larry's] been on fire," Cardinals **wideout** Anquan Boldin told reporters, "running wide open, making big plays. He played like a man among boys."

Now Fitzgerald stood on the sideline, watching the **defense** (DEE-fents) try to keep the Steelers from scoring. He looked at the clock. There was still time left in the game. Could the Cardinals stop them? Who was going to win?

Larry established himself as one of the top college players in the country while playing for the University of Pittsburgh.

Training His Brain

Larry Darnell Fitzgerald Jr. was born on August 31, 1983, in St. Paul, Minnesota. His parents were Carol and Larry Fitzgerald Sr. Carol kept track of health problems in the state. Larry Sr. was a sports reporter. Two years after Larry's birth, his brother, Marcus, was born.

In school, Larry had trouble making good grades. His grandfather, Robert Johnson, was an eye doctor. He had a **vision** (VIH-zhun) clinic in Chicago. Dr. Johnson believed that vision **therapy** (THAYR-uh-pee) would help Larry with his schoolwork. Larry had to stand on a balance beam. He practiced using his hands and eyes to do difficult tasks.

When Larry was twelve, his grandfather added exercises to help him do better at sports. One of them used a rolling pin and a ball hung from the ceiling. The ball had different colored dots on it. The rolling pin had colored stripes. Larry had to touch the dots on the ball with the stripe of the same color on the rolling pin.

Larry says these drills helped him play football. "Anything that helps strengthen your eyes and eye-hand **coordination** [koh-or-dih-NAY-shun] is going to definitely help with catching the ball," he told a reporter for *The Wall Street Journal.*

Something else Larry did as a child would help him later on the field. His father covered sports for the *Minnesota Spokesman-Recorder.* He got Larry a job as a ball boy for the Minnesota Vikings football team.

Dr. Johnson shows how to use his colored rolling pin and baseball.

Larry, former defensive back Phillippi Sparks, and brother Marcus promote "don't text while driving." Marcus also plays football. He is a wide receiver on the California Redwoods, a team in the United Football League.

He watched the Viking players practice, especially Cris Carter and Randy Moss. Both of them were wide receivers. Larry watched as they caught pass after pass. He learned how the football follows different paths depending on how it is thrown. He was training his brain for his future.

Throughout his professional career, a football player is known by the college he attended. Larry will always be known as "Larry Fitzgerald from the University of Pittsburgh."

Getting Started

In his first year of high school, Larry played wide receiver and quarterback. In 1998, at the **Academy** (uh-KAD-uh-mee) of Holy Angels, he started out playing linebacker. Then the coach asked him to play wide receiver. The first time the ball was thrown to him, Larry caught it with just one hand. He scored a touchdown. After that, he never played linebacker again.

Larry was doing well on the field, but his father was still not happy about his grades. He sent Larry to a harder school.

Larry told *The New York Times* that his father was strict. "Anything I did wrong, he was on me. . . . He kind of laid down the law."

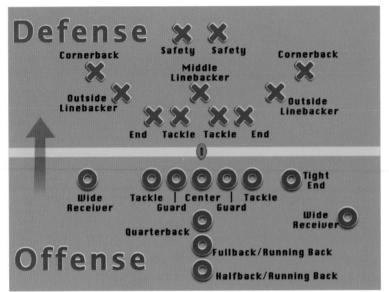

Defense

Cornerback   Safety   Safety   Cornerback

Middle
Linebacker

Outside
Linebacker   Outside
Linebacker

End   Tackle   Tackle   End

Wide
Receiver   Tackle | Center | Tackle   Tight
End
         Guard   Guard

Quarterback   Wide
Receiver

Offense   Fullback/Running Back

Halfback/Running Back

Larry played many positions in school. **On offense** he played quarterback and wide receiver. He also played on defense as a safety and an outside linebacker.

The tough love paid off. In May 2002, Larry graduated from Valley Forge Military Academy in Pennsylvania. Colleges had noticed his football talent. Larry went to college and played for the University of Pittsburgh.

In two years, Larry played 26 games for the Pittsburgh Panthers. He set a school record by scoring 34 touchdowns. That is more than one touchdown per game. He scored 22 of those touchdowns in 2003. Two seasons in a row, he had more than 1,000 receiving yards. He won many awards, including the Walter Camp Award and the Fred Biletnikoff Award. He was the runner-up for the Heisman Trophy, which is held in the highest regard.

While his college career was going well, his personal life was not. He had argued with his mother about a girl he was dating. Feelings were hurt on both sides. Larry and his mother stopped speaking to each other.

He would never get the chance to make it up to her. His mother had breast cancer. She died on April 10, 2003. "He was hurt so much," Larry Sr. told *The New York Times*. "He didn't get to settle some things with her." Larry Jr. still carries her driver's license with him.

After his great football year in 2003, Larry had to make a big decision. Should he stay in school and keep playing college football? Or should he leave school for the NFL?

Sometimes, leaving college for the NFL is a mistake. Staying in school can be a great way to prepare for the NFL.

Larry had always dreamed of playing in the NFL. He felt his time with the Panthers had prepared him well. He decided to make the move.

Was he making a mistake?

On January 10, 2010, the Cardinals beat the Green Bay Packers 51-45 in overtime. Larry scored two touchdowns, which gave him nine touchdowns in his first five playoff games. That was the highest total in NFL history for a player in his first five playoff games.

In the NFL

Larry entered the NFL draft in 2004. The Arizona Cardinals picked him. He was the third college player in the entire country to be selected, which was quite an honor. The coach of the Cardinals, Dennis Green, had been with the Vikings when Larry was a ball boy. Coach Green remembered him.

The Cardinals knew Larry was good. They offered him a six-year contract for $60 million.

The first year in the NFL is very hard for any player. Most NFL teams do not play football like college teams. NFL quarterbacks throw harder. Players are bigger and faster. Defenses are quicker. A college player needs to adjust, and it takes time.

Quarterback Kurt Warner (right) and Fitzgerald plan their next play during the second round of playoffs on January 16, 2010. This time they weren't as fortunate. The New Orleans Saints beat them 45-14 and knocked them out of the playoffs.

In his first year, Larry caught 58 passes and scored 8 touchdowns. It wasn't a bad record, but he felt he could do better.

In his second year, Larry caught 103 passes. That was the most in the NFL. He scored 10 touchdowns. He was named to the

A wide receiver must be alert. At any moment a defensive player could race up and try to knock the ball away. Wide receivers like Larry must be on their guard constantly.

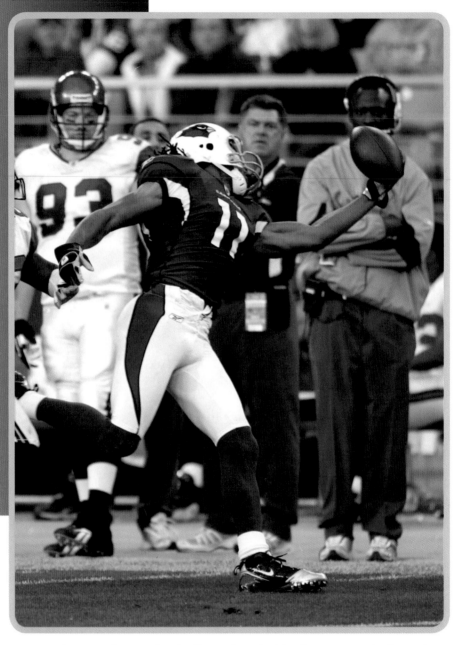

Larry makes catching a football one-handed look easy! His ball-catching ability is the result of years of practice.

Pro Bowl, a game played by the top players in the league.

All this time the Cardinals were getting better. With quarterback Kurt Warner throwing to Larry and his wide-receiving partner Anquan Boldin, and with the great teamwork of other players, the Arizona Cardinals were becoming a good team. Larry caught so many passes, reporters nicknamed him "Sticky Fingers." In 2007 and 2008, he caught for more than 1,400 yards. In 2008 he caught 96 passes and scored 12 touchdowns. One of them was a 78-yard touchdown pass.

In 2008, Fitzgerald also had an outstanding postseason record. In the **championship** (CHAM-pee-un-ship) game against the Philadelphia (fil-uh-DEL-fee-uh) Eagles, he scored three touchdowns in the first half—another record. The Cardinals won 32-25. That victory sent them to their first Super Bowl.

The best players of the year are voted to play in the Pro Bowl. They wear special uniforms for the game, but their regular season team is also shown. If you look closely, you can see the cardinal head—the symbol of the Arizona Cardinals—on Larry's jersey.

Beyond the Super Bowl

The Cardinals defense could not stop the Steelers. Pittsburgh scored a touchdown with just 35 seconds left in the game. They won 27-23.

Larry had mixed feelings about the Super Bowl. The Cardinals didn't win the trophy, but he was glad they had made it that far.

His dad was writing about the game for his newspaper. It was his father's thirtieth year covering the game, but it was the first time a father reported on a Super Bowl that his son was in.

"I can't tell you how remarkable it is to see your son pursue his dreams and realize his **potential** [poh-TEN-shul]," Larry Sr. told

Larry Fitzgerald Sr. interviewed Cardinals running back Edgerrin James and other players when he covered the Super Bowl. Besides writing for newspapers, Larry Sr. is also a reporter for radio, television, and Internet programs.

USA Today. "It's almost hard to believe that it's working out this way."

After the Super Bowl, Larry Jr. was once again voted to play in the Pro Bowl. He caught two touchdown passes. One of them was a 46-yard pass from New Orleans Saints quarterback Drew Brees as the clock ran out in the first half. Larry's team won 30-21, and Larry was named the Pro Bowl's MVP.

Larry's son, Devin Nazario Fitzgerald, was born in 2008. His mother's name is Angela.

One reason Larry catches so many passes is that he can jump very high, often outleaping defensive backs. When you combine his jumping ability with his great hand-eye coordination, it's no wonder he catches so many balls!

In 2009 he had another good season. He caught 97 passes and scored 13 touchdowns. The Cardinals did not return to the Super Bowl, but Fitzgerald was voted to the Pro Bowl for the fifth time in his career. The Cardinals renewed his contract for four years and $40 million.

In the off-season, Fitzgerald follows other dreams. He travels the world and tries new things. In Asia, he rode an elephant. In South America, he went bungee jumping.

He also works to help others. On his web site, he wrote about his mother. He said she worked for many **charities** (CHAYR-ih-teez) in her life. She taught him how important it is to give. When she passed away, Larry started the Carol Fitzgerald **Memorial** (meh-MOR-ee-ul) Fund. It raises money to help people who have HIV/AIDs and breast cancer. He also started the Larry Fitzgerald First Down Fund. It helps children and their families.

After the 2010 Pro Bowl, Fitzgerald traveled to India. He was helping some friends provide hearing aids to children there. "It is pure joy to see the face of a child who is able to hear the sound of a voice for the first time," he wrote on his web site.

In sports it takes hard work to become good and continue to play well. Larry works very hard. He always tries to improve, both as a football player and as a person. He is one of the rising stars of the NFL. His future is one of promise and hope.

CAREER RECEIVING STATISTICS

Year	Team	G	Rec	Yards	Yds/G	Lng	TD	20+	40+	1st	FUM
2009	Arizona	16	97	1,092	68.2	34	13	12	0	69	0
2008	Arizona	16	96	1,431	89.4	78	12	20	5	66	1
2007	Arizona	15	100	1,409	93.9	48	10	19	4	69	3
2006	Arizona	13	69	946	72.8	57	6	11	2	52	0
2005	Arizona	16	103	1,409	88.1	47	10	27	4	67	0
2004	Arizona	16	58	780	48.8	48	8	15	1	36	1
Total		92	523	7,067	76.8	78	86	104	16	359	5

(G = Games, Rec = Receptions, Yards = Receiving Yards, Yds/G = Yards per game, Lng = Longest Reception, TD = Touchdown, 20+ = Receptions of 20 or more yards, 40+ = Receptions of 40 or more yards, 1st = First Downs, FUM = Fumbles)

CHRONOLOGY

1983 Larry Darnell Fitzgerald Jr. is born August 31 in St. Paul, Minnesota.

1985 His brother, Marcus, is born on June 1.

1995 He gets a job as a ball boy for the Minnesota Vikings.

2002 He graduates from Valley Forge Military Academy in Wayne, Pennsylvania. In the fall, he enrolls at the University of Pittsburgh.

2003 After a stellar year at Pittsburgh, he receives the Walter Camp Award, the Paul Warfield Trophy, and the Fred Biletnikoff Award. He is the runner-up for the Heisman Trophy. His mother dies in April; he starts the Carol Fitzgerald Memorial Fund in her honor.

2004 Larry is picked third overall by the Arizona Cardinals in the NFL draft. He signs a six-year, $60 million contract. He starts the Larry Fitzgerald First Down Fund, which provides activities for children as well as computer equipment and vision care.

2005 He is voted to play in the NFL Pro Bowl.

2007 He again plays in the Pro Bowl.

2008 Devin, Larry's son with Angela Nazario, is born. Larry is again invited to play in the Pro Bowl.

2009 He plays in the Super Bowl with the Arizona Cardinals; they are defeated by the Pittsburgh Steelers 27-23. He plays in the Pro Bowl again and is named the game's Most Valuable Player. He signs a four-year, $40 million contract extension. He visits U.S. troops in Iraq.

2010 He is voted to the Pro Bowl again. He travels to India to help fit hearing aids for children with hearing loss.

FIND OUT MORE

Books

Christopher, Matt. *The Super Bowl*. New York: Little, Brown, 2006.

Gilbert, Sara. *The History of the Arizona Cardinals*. Mankato, MN: Creative Education, 2005.

Grabowski, John. *Larry Fitzgerald*. Broomall, PA: Mason Crest Publishers, 2008.

Reinegal, Brady. *Larry Fitzgerald: Pro Bowl Receiver*. Strongsville, OH: Gareth Stevens, 2010.

Sandler, Michael. *Larry Fitzgerald*. New York: Bearport Publishing, 2010.

Works Consulted

Albergotti, Reed. "The NFL's Most Exciting Receiver." *The Wall Street Journal*, January 16, 2009. http://online.wsj.com/article/SB123207803343289089.html

Associated Press. "Fitzgerald Earns MVP at Pro Bowl." February 8, 2009. http://www.azcentral.com/sports/cardinals/articles/2009/02/08/20090208fitzprobowl-ON.html#ixzz0rDHTFOXD

――――. "Fitzgerald Shines as Warner Leads Cardinals to Franchise's First Super Bowl." *ESPN*, January 18, 2009. http://sports.espn.go.com/nfl/recap?gameId=290118022

Bell, Jarrett. "The Bell Tolls: Work, Family Lines Blur for Fitzgerald's Dad." *USA Today*, January 18, 2009. http://www.usatoday.com/sports/football/nfl/2009-01-16-the-bell-tolls_N.htm

Feifer, Jason. "Larry Fitzgerald's Workout: Use Failure as Fuel." *Men's Health*, n.d. http://www.menshealth.com/celebrity-fitness/larry-fitzgerald-fuel

Fitzgerald, Larry, Jr. "Volunteering in India." Larry Fitzgerald: *Travels*, March 31, 2010. http://www.larryfitzgerald11.com/news/volunteering-in-india.html

Fitzgerald, Larry, Sr. "The Mitchell Report―Pass the Asterisks Around." *Minnesota Spokesman-Recorder*, December 27, 2007. http://www.larry-fitzgerald.com/articles/The-Mitchell-report-pass-the-asterisks-around.htm

Klis, Mike. "MVP to Mend Broken Thumb," *Denver Post*, February 9, 2009. http://www.denverpost.com/sports/ci_11660421

LaPointe, Joe. "One Step from Super Bowl, Fitzgerald Is Suddenly an Open Book." *The New York Times*, January 18, 2009. http://www.nytimes.com/2009/01/18/sports/football/18cardinals.html

"Larry Fitzgerald Off the Field." http://www.larryfitzgerald11.com/off-the-field.html

McManaman, Bob. "Fitzgerald's Hands Elevate His Status." *The Arizona Republic*, January 28, 2009. http://www.azcentral.com/sports/cardinals/articles/2009/01/28/20090128sb-fitzhands0129.html

Rock, Tom. "NFC Championship Game: Better Beware of Fitzgerald." *Newsday*, January 17, 2009. http://larry-fitzgerald.com/jr/index.php?option=com_content&task=view&id=132&Itemid=2

On the Internet

Arizona Cardinals
   http://www.azcardinals.com

Larry Fitzgerald Jr. Official Web Site
   http://www.larryfitzgerald11.com

Larry Fitzgerald Sr. Official Web Site
   http://www.larry-fitzgerald.com

NFL Player: Larry Fitzgerald
   http://www.nfl.com/players/larryfitzgerald/profile?id=FIT437493

GLOSSARY

academy (uh-KAD-uh-mee)—Private high school.

championship (CHAM-pee-un-ship)—A game or series of games to determine a champion.

charity (CHAYR-ih-tee)—A group of people who donate time and money to help those who are in need.

coordination (koh-or-dih-NAY-shun)—The ability to control how different parts of the body move so that they all work well together.

defense (DEE-fents)—In football, the players who try to keep the other team from scoring.

memorial (meh-MOR-ee-ul)—Something created to honor someone who died.

National Football League (NASH-uh-nul FUT-bol LEEG)—The professional football league in the United States.

offense (AH-fents)—In football, the players who try to score against the other team.

official (oh-FIH-shul)—In sports contests, a person who enforces the rules of the game.

opponents (uh-POH-nunts)—The teams who are playing against one another.

potential (poh-TEN-shul)—A measure of what is possible.

quarterback (KWOR-ter-bak)—The player on a football team who leads the offense.

spike (SPYK)—To slam the ball into the ground.

Super Bowl—An annual football game played in the United States that determines which team is the champion of the NFL.

therapy (THAYR-uh-pee)—Treatment for a medical condition.

vision (VIH-zhun)—Sight.

wideout (WYD-out)—Another term for *wide receiver.*

wide receiver (ree-SEE-ver)—A football player who catches passes.

INDEX